Neon Moons

Also by Angela Johnson and published by Ginninderra Press
No Stories, No Songs
Endlessly Passing

Angela Johnson
Neon Moons

Acknowledgements

Some of these poems have been published in
Gang Gang, Five Bells, Centoria, Yellow Moon
and Central Coast Poets Anthologies

To my daughters
Susan, Julie and Vicki

Neon Moons
ISBN 978 1 74027 284 1
Copyright © Angela Johnson 2004

First published 2004
Reprinted 2016

Ginninderra Press
PO Box 3461 Port Adelaide 5015
www.ginninderrapress.com.au

Contents

Impasto	7
The Metal Heart	8
Almost Eden	10
Remnant Pools	13
Roadside	15
Outback	16
Haiku	17
Tanka	18
Contact	19
The Nullarbor	21
Summer Rain	22
Dreams	23
Blackberries (1)	24
Blackberries (2)	25
The Wreck	26
Searching	27
Tracks	28
Anzacs	29
Journey	30
Nightlife	31
Cool Change	32
Watching	33
Sigh	34
A Different Beat	35
The Love Wraith	36
Old Head	38
Roses	39
Dark Dreams	40
Cinquain	41
Isobel	42
Mouths of Babes	44

Assimilation	45
Refugees in Rooms (1945)	46
Asunder	47
In the Mountains	48
Blank Canvas	49
Canticle	50
Closure	51
The Aunt	52
Summer Night	54
Child	55
No Stories No songs	56
The Offering	57
Triolet	58
Fledgling	60
A Day Trip to a Greek Island	61
Neon Moons	63
Woman in a garden	64
The Sitter	65
Winter	66
Belated	67
Venice	68
After Venice	70
Bloodlines	71
My Street	72
Magnetic Resonance Imaging	73
Sea Lover	74
Ashes: In a New Land	75
Sacred Ibis	76
Near Dorrigo	77
Perfection	78
Pictures in a Mining Museum	79
Boat People	80
Honey	81
Last Word	82

Impasto

Caged – duty-bound – blinkered.
Persuasions to revisit pleasures drone like a dull song.
So I could have missed
an outrageous country day –
missed a pizza and the works day.

Zipping down a carrion highway past long-parched gullies –
distant trees, scatter
a confetti of cockatoos
into a blue sky
lashed with whipped-cream clouds –

and I savour the sweet fragrance
squeezed from the eucalypts
by a fierce heat.

Then I yield to this sunburnt-country day.

The Metal Heart

Going…going.
Under the truck's bonnet
the metal heart ticks on.

Marvel, as hot tyres
suck the road under,
how the snail-house trails behind effortlessly.
Inching along at 100 ks
there's barely a mark on the map after a day's slog.
Going…going.
Ticking off limitless miles
of yellow-grassed cattle stations,
lifeless
in the baking heat,
past roadside crows perched on carrion.

Shuddering over dirt tracks
through opaline ranges
where determined trees
dig deep,

we are dwarfed
in bunched landforms
and ancient mosaic gorges.
We find deep dark water
hanging white over rock ledges.

And going on,
weary of harsh beauty,
we look for gentler land,
where red-dusted sheep
file through young spinifex.

And the metal heart beats
for home.

Almost Eden

1

The borrowed ute creaked from the kerb
of the silent street.
In the tray, the children lay sleeping,
limp as rag dolls, on still-warm blankets.

Past darkened terraces
where aunts slept, unconcerned.
Past the great iron fence of the cemetery,
and the already forgotten forebears.
Beside a trundling night tram,
yellow-lit around a lone conductor.
Past all their young days
so far.

Miles away, they woke
to the soft conversation
of distant doves.

2

New bungalows speckled once-lush fields,
and thickened towards the hub;
hemmed in their old weatherboard,
paint-hungry, a survivor.

Their longing faded,
then like bees on scented air
they roamed – camera eyes
capturing the glare of footpaths,
new, hopscotch-ready,
and cloned houses,
with smooth, room-sized lawns.

3

Where a path curves,
from locked wire gate to front door,
someone's grandfather kneels,
supplicant,
before a border of vivid annuals.

The circle of his grey felt hat
shadows his shoulders,
and the satin vest across his back
reflects the sun.
In a shaded corner beneath shrubs,
a sprinkler ticks.

Behind a porch,
the window's lace curtains
hang heavy, luscious;
blinds half-drawn – dismissive,
like the half-drawn lids of eyes.

> Unaware of comparisons,
> they wore their pallid skin and ratty hair
> with innocence,
> and thrived.
>
> Then, when the privet thickened the air,
> and the sweet, vanilla smell of oleander
> welcomed summer,
> like pups, they nosed the air
> at the sea salt
> windborne up the North Road,
> where blue beach days beckoned.

Remnant Pools

(The Great Depression, Victoria, 1937)

To the north by clattering train,
then jauntily on frog-green trams,
in dreams we returned to our planet,
unnourished suburb
tucked against a depleted city.

Terrace rows stand saw-toothed
against the sky,
or in winter, parading chimneys
breathe smoke arabesques.

In dull rooms, fallen flesh of walls,
bare, skeletal laths
ignored by women who finger rosaries
of born-again wrinkled wool
and dwell on tomorrow's succour.

Shabby havens where infants
sense the silent huddle
that denies the listening rent-man.
Where men study form
while hope is dashed
by the wireless's rising whine.

In summer,
children leave narrow verandas
to range barefoot in streets
and digging, find beauty
in the black glitter of liquid tar
on hot footpaths.

Or we would clamber from small yards,
through motley gates and fences,
to wonder, and whisper secrets,
in lanes of everlasting bluestone,
where, on a night after rain,
we saw the moon
multiplied in remnant pools.

Roadside

Elusive birds, swift as comets
trace the air between roadside trees.

Straining to see
spirited antics hidden in leaves,

I stand still;
listen to furtive rustling overhead.

Once, a small dead bird
lay in grass beside my feet

and my cautious hands reached down;
touched parasol ribs, beneath still wings.

Outback

Sand yields to churning tyres.
It holds the fate of drivers
who urge hot-revved trucks
to firm ground.

It flows back,
impervious to the thrust
of the convoy
and the smug men
who fold their arms
and imagine they are victorious.

Haiku

1

Naked the tree stands
deep circled in fallen leaves
waiting for Spring's touch.

2

Between roadside trees
birds trace the air like comets
to reach new blossoms.

Tanka

1

The rain-wet garden
where fronds decant their burden
reflects in small pools.
You can hear the drip and ping
of raindrops on metal.

2

On the dark shore's dunes
creatures huddled in shadows
see the moon rising.
It lights a curved path
to the crystal-faced rock pools.

Contact

NO STOPPING AT ANY TIME.

An urban sign on an outback road
ignored by Koori men
in cattlemen's hats.

Under the high sun
we braked in trepidation;
questioned the need to stop.

A young man draped his arms –
leaned in a head of curls,
fine face slack with drink.

'Where you goin'?
'When you come back?'

'Kata Tjuta,' I said,
currying favour,
having a stab at his language.

It cut no ice, duplicity recognised.
'You got drink, boss?
'I can pay, boss.' Dignity intact.

'Sorry, mate.'
Refusals steeped in falsity,
voice uncertain, coaxing almost;
lying, mate.

A breath's wait,
his hand extended – accepting.
'Give hand, boss.'

I watched two hands reaching,
clasping, and thought of
token hands on rock walls

or planted in city parks,
but not real and warm
with a man's blood.

Mute, we continued past sighing desert oaks
while bottled wine cooled
in the ticking fridge.

The Nullarbor

The Nullarbor turns to the night
to take its share of lunar light.

Silence spreads like heavy wings
on stunted shrubs – harbouring
sleep-numbed birds – huddling.

The moon-white highway splits the plain,
a truck's roar ebbs and swells again.
Then as the silence folds back in

the Nullarbor turns to the night
to take its share of lunar light.

Summer Rain

As the dense summer rain spills
from skies thick with dark clouds,
the garden runs rampant.
Heavy branches bar my path
and decant their wet burden.

The steady drip of rain
on rotting leaves and iron

is a rhythm for spent flowers
that float
down a new-formed stream
and mass at an iron grate –
then, held together, squeeze through.

Dreams

Why do you visit my dreams,
hide in others' bodies?
You can't trick me now.

Rarely do I think of you
in waking days.
I would cringe at the folly of
old emotions

insincere in the moment;
more like drunks on a binge,
enjoying the pain.

So, why do you visit my dreams?

Blackberries (1)

In communal wellies
we clumped, snake-ignorant,
to the blackberry gully,
where autumn advertised
and a myriad suns
glittered from dark drupels.

Brimful,
dented billies swung
beside thorned flesh
drizzled scarlet
while
beneath warm sun and bird babble,
eager fingers stained fruit-purple.

Also this day,
transient as shadows,
memories were gathered.

Blackberries (2)

Sun-brittle paddocks
wrapped the house,
and birds waited in trees.

Inside, woodsmoke seeped,
and trapped flies
muttered in the curtains.

The woman stirred the berries,
bubbling and pink-frothed
at the pot's edge,

or, tongue clamped,
bent to fuel the stove's
orange gape.

Ample
in patterned pinny she ruled
magic with industry
to wax-seal each dark jar.

The Wreck

The sea, like an orca with a seal pup,
hurled the ship to the shore.

Now rust-eaten – embedded.
Life scuttles in mothering bones
ghosted by the visiting moon,

a witness to the insistent return
of the sea – a false penitent
whose waves clutch, impotent,
against sucking sand.

The wind moans a lament through iron lace,
an echo of the cries
that once trembled towards the stars.

Searching

the hours
fly by
while I
dwell on
days gone

concepts
abate
I can't
create
a thought
that's new

time ticks
rhythmic
be quick

construct
a game
to stir
my brain
invent a ruse
to find
the muse

Tracks

Motionless:
Cattle on hell-hot gibber.

Choreographed heads turn
and watch
dust-drenched autos
on a quest.

Beyond brown beast and stones,
distant ranges hover
above a trembling horizon,
and blurred, stunted trees
blue-float on haze rivers.

Encapsulated
in four-by-four heaven,
drivers shudder on day-long tracks
towards evenings
of self-congratulations.

Anzacs

Below the dark earth, bone on bone,
soldiers lie buried far from home.

Persuaded that the cause was just,
their blood was spilled; their weapons rust.

Did they recall the children's game
when friend and foe pretended pain,

when flags on sticks were held up high
for gallant heroes, marching by?

Each year, in early morning pallor,
sombre mourners praise their valour.

And underneath the circling moon,
bone lies on bone in earth's dark tomb.

Journey

Together they travel,
the train tracking steadily.
She knows:
his destination is evident
in the bones, barely fleshed
in the taut, pallid skin.

She crochets,
he pens a crossword –
serenity wraps them.

She thinks of her earlier selves,
locked within.
How each one holds
a remnant of the other –
a set of Russian dolls.

She folds her work,
touches his arm –
soon they will arrive.

Nightlife

At night when the house settles
and objects slink into shadow,
I sleep, curled like a comma.

Dreams hover; old film flickering,
sensuous, fleeting,
or Gothic and dark-grained.

Heavy flesh struggles to surface
and a scream suffocates
at the dry gape of my mouth.

I watch the fading night
and delude myself
that I am not this dream's author.

Cool Change

Humidity stifles
heat presses down.

Motionless garden
silent the house.

Soft as a moth wing
uncertainly felt

a cool breath descends
raindrops are dealt.

Wind pushes harder
trees come alive

branches toss leaves
to spiralling rain

coaxing sweet scent
from freshening air.

Tension diminished
house timbers creak.

Clouds brush the moon
the earth breathes deep.

Watching

The chaste scent of a rose pricks memory.
A house in a garden. I am a cub,
watching the shuttling of the pride.

I want to pluck from images
the lessons learned.

Instead, I hear the china clink
of gathered eggs –
see the technicolour of bordered flowers
and remember – always
there was the scent of roses.

Sigh

Sigh, desert oaks
over miles between ranges.
Sigh me the song
you have sung down the ages.

Lament with the lover,
                the mother, the fool;
sigh for the dreamer,
                the too beautiful.

Keen for the ghettoed,
who can't hear you sing,
or even the rich man,
who has everything:
and wonders…why he sighs.

A Different Beat

When he came to the door
he was dressed for the part;
arms full of florist's flowers.

She answered the door
dressed to kill. The slinky dress,
the salesgirl had said, 'is so you'.

After some chit-chat he held her.
She hoped her perfume
was enticing.

Mentally, he measured
the distance
to the bedroom.

Together, skin on skin,
they had a magnificent time
as the flowers wilted.

Later, it became clear
they were not reading
from the same script.

The Love Wraith

Love is a wraith.
It beckoned me
to many destinations.

It spurned my grey-mouse mother,
who'd had truck with it.
Wooed me
from father's tobacco-scented shirt;
the cosy laps of aunts.

First stop: the magic of picture shows
and Shirley Temple dimpling,
impossible fairy tales
with happy endings.

Later, with a coquette's guile,
more delights of the silver screen;
slick lovers in tuxedos
bent over wax-faced beauties
whose lashes cast
shadows on flawless cheeks.

For the older me,
city shop windows
full of sightless brides –
fragile veils floating;

but the youth on offer
were no match for a girl on a mission.

So, hand in hand,
the wraith and I spiralled
into shadowy rooms
where reality sniggered in a corner.

Then I caught it looking in a mirror,
questioning love.

Old Head

Oh,
how I want
to prick your bubble.

Motive insinuates
intelligence.

Fact is,
this is an urge
to purge myself

of the power
I have

to clear your eyes
before
lovers arise.

Roses

Roses from the garden, picked
Heedless of flesh fiercely pricked,
Dominate familiar rooms,
Woo the light on every bloom.

Float their fragrance all around,
Rule the room without a sound.
Gifts from lovers, to persuade,
Cause all colours near to fade.

Soon their stems will slowly shrink.
The prima donnas cannot drink
Fragrance, colour; light has flown.
Soon they'll scatter and be gone.

Dark Dreams

Curled like a comma, I watched myself sleep,
and saw without looking, a small visitant.
Its mission was clear, that I was its choice.
I called out for help with a silent voice.
Then smiling a smile I will never forget,
it lay down behind me, as cold as ice.

Cinquain

Dreams
sensuous   ominous
creep   threaten   flicker
a   grainy   Gothic   movie
nightmare

Isobel

As still as a cub
camouflaged in shadows
my small child squats.

Rapt, she listens and peers
through the slots of a drain
where water whispers.

Her arms, fine as reeds,
hug twig knees –
her dress trails in leaves.

I am not mimicked here.
In a contest I could not win,
Norse genes were claimed for her –

apparent in alabaster skin
and frothed hair,
paler than gold.

Like a plant filmed in time lapse
I see her grown –
the thicken and push of bone

within pearl-taut flesh,
a destiny planned, yet unknown.
My thoughts are halted

by a blue, primal stare.
Performing,
she springs in the air,

then shrieking with laughter,
strafes the garden
to nowhere in particular.

Mouths of Babes

O my sweet one,
whose infant head
nuzzled my neck
while
we danced the floor,
attempted
the lyrics of a song he
'wouldn't poke a stick at' now,
made the observation
all old women look alike.

While reluctantly
seeing
his point of view,
I disregarded
the impulse
towards spiky red hair
and eyebrow jewels,
knowing somewhere
there is some song
we will sing together.

Assimilation

I discovered
grandmother was a foreigner.

Irrelevant, that her speech was accent-free
or her amber-eyed sons Celtic-fair.

It was obvious.
I should have known –

questioned her dark skin,
the long marks on her ears,

where heavy earrings
had once hung.

Then, choosing apples in a shop,
she laughed and spoke in a different tongue.

Years later,
I wonder what I heard.

Refugees in Rooms (1945)

From the top of the stairs looking down
you could see the black telephone
on the lamp-lit table.

A circle of doors tucked in shadow
were closed like vaults – blotting sound
until opened furtively by men who crept,
grey as ghosts.

When the house stretched to a new day,
the telephone on the table rang
but the doors remained closed, and the stairs empty.

Asunder

The sun's breath rocked the blind gently
behind the heavy curtain.
In an earlier room, a paler sun defined
thin-legged boys in tennis whites,
come to take leave of their mother.

A queen,
she keeps a decent distance,
with tucked chin
or proffered cheek;
but pride escapes from her eyes.

Sisters, with hair at the beck of butterfly clips
crunch scissors through organdie,
ready to cut loose – to find a different love.
Distant from the house,
the father potters in his shed.

His fingers yearn
over seedlings that promise pleasure.
The smoke from his pipe
curls above shelved flagons,
empty of solace.

Inside the door,
one-way liaison with the house,
a bell dangles on a cord.
He will be summoned
for meals.

In the Mountains

Autumn steals under summer's guard
fresh as a new love;
brushes the air cool, the sunlight
with a lighter palette.

Promises clear days never-ending;
flaunts a canvas – a camouflage
of brazen colour
that blusters at inevitable winter.

Blank Canvas

She walks towards me –
a mark between roadside trees.
I watch – waiting for a sign
that we share the same landscape.

Today she is blue and yellow.
In a painting,
she would merge with the scene –
but here she is separate
from it and me.

She speaks soothingly,
impossibly understands everything;
only later
reflection winnows a possible barb.

We toss words, flimsy as confetti,
across the space between us.

How little I see of her now.

Yet once, she came to my door,
a newcomer
seeking a shoulder.

Canticle

The old sea wall
crusted, moon-visited,
a dream-drenched altar

defines a moment
or a direction.

Holds the secret of
its origins and
repels a capricious sea.

In moist crevices,
nurtures sea creatures.

Closure

The house awaits demolition.
No study or guest room with en-suite.

Yet once, in the breath of new timber,
a family managed the human huddle
with equanimity; kept separate
the tracks of their emotions.

A dormitory of lanky boys
crept between the ice-white sheets
of beds on a gauzed-in veranda
and slept to the grunt of distant cattle.

Sisters – privileged
in the intimacy of a shared room,
grew as different as their dreams.

The house seasoned to the clock's tick;
quivered to the thump of running feet;
the rhythmical slap of the screen door.

>Dousing smokes, the gang begins
>to rip weather boards and the flesh of walls
>to the blare of a truck's wireless.
>
>When they stop,
>the frame stands bare,
>and the dust drizzles like rain
>on the forgotten roses.

The Aunt

She ruled
her mother's kitchen,
surfaces scrubbed
bone-clean.

A dark rose,
long-stemmed,
nearing full bloom.

Pictures spill
from a box,
soft with age;

her arms hooped
around
this child or that.

we, curious,
were fobbed off
with dubious tales:

'Should have married Jack,'
they said
of our difficult father.

We remember visiting:
bath time;
strong arms lifting, towelling;

then
hair twisted
in rag curlers;

and special days
lining up
to parfait glasses,
brimful,
and the long spoons dipping.

Summer Night

Our eyes mirrored sequined trawlers
skimming the wind-scuffed bay,
arms outstretched like dancers.

Heedless of the frenzy in relentless nets,
we sensed a sailor's comfort
from the flick of red to green
on channel markers   beckoning,

and stood on the shoreline
where the waves slapped,
lamenting the last boat's silent glide
behind the night-dark headland.

Child

Honeysuckle-sweet
against my breast,
eyes wide – alert,
or in arcs of sleep.

Awareness emerges
to kindle your fear.
Fairy-tale truths fail
to ease your pain.
Still you cling.

I lost your touch
to a fan of reaching hands,
trusted your endurance.
Now your guarded eyes
deflect my heart.

Adrift, I will float above rooftops
like a Chagall bride
with my wand of flowers.

No Stories No songs

The photograph is old, portrays a man;
the woman clinging to his arm, her string of beads

are strangely brave. Also, two children, another soon.
It doesn't show the dingy house, the hunger ghost.

The table with newspaper cloth, his angry swipe
that hurls the pot and spills the tea.

The spilt glitter of white sugar turning brown,
the children's anguished cries, the woman's cringe.

It doesn't show the good nights when he played the wag,
kids hanging to his shirt through house and yard;

or how he took them on his knee to sing them songs,
and put them in their bed, small limbs entwined,

or why she told no stories, sang no songs.

The Offering

Sand gloved our hands.
The paddles were heavy;
hard to balance.

As we walked up the beach,
the afternoon sun
orange at our backs,

I waited for you to speak,
to lead.
The path was steep.

Near the crest,
you found time
to snatch some flowers.

I held them
like a lifeline
all the way home.

How could I know
when I touched your skin,
it would be so cold
I would shiver forever?

Triolet

1

Yachts lie at anchor on the bay,
rock gently with the ebb and flow;
while the orange dying of the day
paints yachts at anchor on the bay.

On water where the shore lights sway
in silhouette, two sailors row
through yachts at anchor on the bay,
together with the ebb and flow.

2

The water dawdles at the edge
of tangled scrub where creatures hide
in trees or on a rock's dark ledge
where water dawdles at the edge.

A scurry in the dampened sedge,
a scavenger will beat the tide
where water dawdles at the edge
in tangled scrub where creatures hide.

3

He loosed the bounty of my hair.
It fell upon his honey wrist,
and often I'd remember where
he loosed the bounty of my hair.

In gardens where the trees were bare,
though it was not a lover's tryst,
he loosed the bounty of my hair.
It fell upon his honey wrist.

Fledgling

The beauty of
embered hair on pale shoulders,
hunched – a screen flickering.

Newly fledged, her 'child' trails
her mirror
invites comparisons.

She unwinds
to the present – smiles,
bright and confident.

If confidence brittle as ice
can be shattered
by innocence or falsity

when she seeks answers,
who will be her sage?

A Day Trip to a Greek Island

The hollow cats, both beggar and thief,
lurking near tourist ships
aren't from central casting.
The cool, white air picking at my shirt,
arousing the skin beneath;
real enough.

But the local boats along the quay,
going nowhere,
painted perfectly
to the tip of their curlicue bows,
opposite boutiques, artfully echoing
Paris or Chapel Street;

the hillside houses'
fresh, white sameness
in laneways thick with
                T-shirt vendors,
                      sit oddly

with images of
troubled ex-pat writers toiling
in digs with 'character',
ducking out to breathe the air;
buy the hard-earned bread.

On an old bus, we escape
to the other side of the island,
where the ocean laps, clean and deep,
against rock ledges,
so fishing boats come straight in

with the day's catch
and Greeks come,
               arms outstretched,
                           jostling for the 'pick'.

Returning,
the bus passes
a goat tethered in a barren landscape,
and a solitary taverna
where men are gathering.

The main game is winding up, quayside,
and the hollow cats slink off as ships leave.

Neon Moons

The city looms over attached suburbs
harbouring children.

From the train,
high beside table-top backyards,
you can see them at play,
and gathering in back lanes.

Night and day, high-rise glitters
so darkness approaches unnoticed.

Fumes swirl, to the swish of cars leaving;
neons fidget on duco – flash on faces.

A half-quiet descends. A girl,
a child's drawing,
with echidna hair and stick legs,
shuffles her booted feet, waiting for the lights.

Hugging herself, she runs to the underground,
past remnant buskers winding up.

Look (you could call),
where streets slice the city,
how dust settles on trees collared in bitumen,

while new life waits for the beck of spring,
even as leaves fall to autumn;
and children are happy with their neon moons.

Woman in a garden

For days I have watched
the way she drifts from
house to garden.

I distrust my curiosity;
wonder what motivates
my need to talk to her;

berate myself, a voyeur,
and return to a fiction of her,
furtive or garrulous

in far-off market places.
When women visit, I hear
their crystal laughter rising.

Later, children play and squabble;
are constrained by a man's voice,
consonant rich.

In the garden this morning,
for the first time in weeks
the grass was wet.

It drenched her trailing skirt.
She bent to free her ankles,
and drops of dew from blossoms

spilled into her hair.
When she stood, the sunlight
lit them like diamonds.

The Sitter

You are unaware:

lamplight paints your profile,
tips over your shoulder
and the rise of your breasts.

I prepare an imaginary canvas;
mix warm skin tones;
consider the rich glint of the bracelet.

I re-acquaint myself with your face,
background shadows in umber and violet
flicked with yellow;   and your hands

that dark depth between fingers,
the fragility of bone,
the elusive journey of veins.

I've seen you hold a baby's head
the way you hold your book,
cupped in one hand.

The other, arced, is ready to turn the page.
Then you look up – rise;
leave me with a loaded brush.

Winter

It's no use
blaming
the crumpled foil sea,
or the passive
dark clouds, hung low.

You lost your colours
long before this grey day.
See how the curious bird
points its yellow eye
in your direction? Look

at the way it spreads its wings
then lifts,
legs trailing,
and marks itself stark-white
between sea and sky.

Belated

Last night I spoke with a dead man;
belatedly put the question,
'Did you love her?'

His remembered voice – hearty, yet hesitant;
    'Yes – yes I did, I did.'
A breath brushed the window's gauze

and the ice-chip stars
flicked their ancient signals,
failing to trivialise my sorrow.

Venice

I'm not prepared for this
press of flesh,
the massed murmuring
together with
the layered rhetoric of tourist guides,
rising to the great vault
then echoing down.

I'm blind
to the beauty of the Pala d'Oro,
dumb before the ancient mosaics.
I long to escape to the piazza,
watch the Moors beat time,
the tethered gondolas rock.

*

This evening, there is rain.
Sergio's resonant voice
mocks his elfin frame.
'Signora, come.'

He taps the phone,
waves away my reluctance
to speak his language,
punctuates my crippled words
with allora, allora.

*

In my room,
timber shutters open
above a rain-washed courtyard.

In half-light, vines reach up walls
and a slender cat
loiters on the wet path.

I whisper,   puss – puss,
and wait for the upturn
of its Carnevale face.

After Venice

The train clatters into Genoa,

Venice already a memory,
Byzantine-beautiful with water at her feet;
waves of suitors seeking
her mercantile heart in travel packs.

Above the city port, once her rival, the car strains
through mountains, sharp as witches hats.

At the summit, a village bears our name.
I wonder aloud, why they left. 'The mountains,
you see,' they shrug. 'Farms too small.'

There is a feast, and I recognise, or imagine
a likeness
in a colour and slant of eye; a mouth's curve.

The old church is locked – its roof ruined,
so only God and the seasons may enter.

The graves' tenants are re-interred
into cubicles, marble-faced
and bedecked with photos and plastic flowers.
I ask, 'Where is Francesco's grave?'

In a cold room, a lid lifted from the floor, reveals
a jumble of fragile, yellowed bones and two skulls.

A gesture tells me, I may choose my patriarch.

Bloodlines

Like any herd, in fact, sheltered
in the dense shade of leaves and bracts,
they knew the value of a tree.

The blue-checked shirts and moleskins
defined their breed,
gathered there to talk bloodlines.

Their proper women spurn a uniform,
discreetly approach fashion's boundary,

confident in their genealogy of shared names,
through enhanced couplings, just like any herd.

My Street

My street runs east and west.
Most mornings when I walk
        I head east into the sun.

Today   my eyes wept in the glare.
A figure walked towards me
        with the sun at its back.

It must have been God.
A spectacular corona surrounded
the silhouette   I was fearful.

I didn't know how to genuflect –
pretended it must be a neighbour
    and smiling weakly
        slantwise
            hurried on.

Magnetic Resonance Imaging

The white robe is a shroud.
Its impersonal odour fits the circumstance.
The cramped cubicle is expected,
but my earrings on the bench surprise;
perfect circles of gold light.

The body works, after a fashion;
the heart pumps blood,
the feet pad quietly
toward the attendant.

Masked, I can feign sleep,
choose where to place my arms
on the narrow slab
as it creeps into the capsule.
My fingers clasp the lifeline buzzer
against my diaphragm.

Rap rhythms clatter;
slice images of tissue and bone
others will decipher.
Though something stamped this flesh;
gave me my colours.

I hustle memory,
search beyond images
for a chink of understanding.

Sea Lover

Your voice is seductive,
a whisper
reaching my bed.

Other nights you moan;
edge towards torment,
or rage at rock faces,

dragging into you
the wet-edged earth
you must visit again
                    and again.

If I drown in you,
will you rock me forever?

Ashes: In a New Land

'A plain white bowl is what I need,'
she'd said.
The memory touched down,
futile as her puppet legs, negotiating the rubble.

It's nothing new, this picking over,
piecing together lives from ruins.
Then, answers were found in ancient feuds;
here there is no answer.

Already, spiders' webs glint;
drape from blackened bricks
across gaps that had been windows.

At the shelter, she'd held children – felt
the tender architecture of their bones
against her woman's body;
watched the fires' light make paintings
of faces in the dark.

She wants to be brave.
Everywhere smoke drifts
and she is frozen in ashes.

Sacred Ibis

A frieze on a ledge;
scimitar beaks sheathed
inside warm wings.

The sun's early rays tint them
flamingo pink.

Their preening surprises with its grace
before the short, floppy flight down
to breakfast on the tip.

A later light discloses
soiled scavengers
with flakey skin on bald heads.

It's a crime scene, the way
they plod together, stabbing the refuse.

Sated,
they will fly to a nearby lake,
not quite like the ancient Nile,

where Thoth, god of writing,
visited earth in their guise,
proclaimed them sacred,
to be buried with kings;

and Artemis, goddess of the moon,
bathed them milk-white
in her image.

Near Dorrigo

The valley is a dense, deep blue;
fathomless.
There is no sound.
It's a moment
when forgiveness seems possible,
though frivolous
here, where you can see forever
and, far below, birds swim in circles
like spirits questing.

Perfection

The forest is quiet as imagined death.
No leaf falls. Shadows freeze,
sun patches on the track, unruffled.

Suppress breath and listen.
Wouldn't it be folly to move?

A bird clings to a tree-trunk,
its plain colour
so natural in the bush.

It will be gone
before you complete your next step.

Could you capture it,
cradle it softly in your hand?
Then
you would feel a heartbeat
through the mesh of ribs and feathers.

Its identity can be found in a book.
Here on the tree, where it scans
with a black-speck eye,
it is perfect.

Pictures in a Mining Museum

Dusty floors and mock daylight
diminish contrasts,
enhance
the grey exhibits.

Rectangles of paper on walls;
a world of clans,
grouped chattels
and limp clothing in glass cases.

Only surgical instruments
attest
to once-flesh people.

Cracks mar a photograph of
ladies parading in a garden.
Elegant heads balance grand hats
above faces
blank as mannequins.

Arranged according to rank
in diminishing perspective
their embroidered skirts trail.

Formal in black
officials stand proudly beside the boss
who lolls in his chair
deigns the image
denying the fellowship they affect,

Framed against a backdrop of machines
tousle-haired miners
squint into the sun.

Boat People

The air is gauze, coolly wrapped,
and a scent of recent flowers wafts
where this dormitory of sleepers
were tucked into their eternity
an eternity ago.

Structures have softened;
are lichen-patterned and worn.
Down straight paths,
weeds' pink flowers quiver,
and crucifix shadows
twist in the sun.

(From all corners they slow-sailed,
coerced by dreams or desperation;
felt a dumb resignation
as the hard earth rose to their first step;
        trailed like ants into their lives,
surprised at the tenacity of old bonds.)

Still, someone visits, owns these names,
wonders.   Now rain speckles the stone,
gathers volume on a cold angel
and drips from the wingtips.

Honey

Suburbs of wattle;
it droops
thick and yellow.
Fecund blossoms
open
to the lust of bees
burying in.

Giddy with thrum
they swarm
to nectar land.

In Africa
acres of plastic shelters
ebony young
desperate
at dry breasts.
Where is their honey?
Are there no bees?

Eyes weep more than tears.

Last Word

I cannot say
how difficult it was
to leave you.

I have not allowed
my heart to break.

www.ingramcontent.com/pod-product-compliance
Lightning Source LLC
Chambersburg PA
CBHW062146100526
44589CB00014B/1712